# In Celebration of the Death of Faeries

by Marilyn Wolf

Dedicated to the men who refused to take care of me

and forced me to grow up.

# Table of Contents

You have come to our group as a guest
                                    with a friend.
We members greet each other with the usual hugs
                                    and kisses.

The meeting starts.
We listen.
It ends.

The wine flows.
The hugs increase.
The kisses lengthen.

I notice you do not join us.

In the midst of a kiss
        You take my arm and pull me away.

            Unique approach.

You say, "You have the longest legs in the room."
Sounds good;
There's a guy 6' 4" here
Must be a line.

Another glass of wine.

The wine is letting me just enjoy you
I don't try to analyze you, now.

I make a pass at you,
            You ask me why.

            Why?

        No one ever asked before.

Maybe you're worth really getting to know.

I never knew what to call it
    Until you taught me to "skim."

causing no displacement

see new things
    with less effort

Like running on just the tips of the grass.

And your soul starts to dance.
    gently, slowly,
    then faster.

never actually out of control.


Just skimming.

My friends say I've grown hard
                    jaded
                    cynical
                    tough.
I protect myself efficiently
                thoroughly
                often.
Except with my kids
                and you.

Please, don't abuse my soul.

I'm here on time.
I only have an hour.

When we planned it, that seemed like plenty.
      Time to talk.
      Have some coffee.

I call to see if you have left.
Naked under your bathrobe.
      Unshowered,
      Playing with your kids,
I hear your voice fall when I tell you what time it is.

You promise faithfully to be here in twenty minutes.

You come in thirty-five.

I watch you walk in.
      Strong,
            self-assured,
            handsome,
            sexy
                  (I love the way you walk.)
                 I'm glad I get to be seen with you.

      I feel your leg against mine.
      Watch your beard move as you talk.

Disappointed the time is so short.

The loving's over
>And we're thirsty.

You walk down the hallway.
I watch.


The light as you approach:

>shines through your hair
>>(mussed from the pillows)

>makes your shoulder muscles prominent
>>(where I laid my arm)

>completely shadows the small of your back
>>(where I held you with my hands)

>brings a paler shadow to your buttocks
>>(so nice next to my knee)

>causes your legs to alternately give and receive shadows
>>(I still feel them under my feet)


The light passes over your head and falls down your back
>like summer rain

When it is behind you
And that handsome body is in full view,

I am glad to be thirsty.

As I come in the door, my body feels your kiss---
      My soul feels your distance.

Oh, yes…Your kids are here.

You find it hard to be a Lover and a Parent.
      Parent wins.

We all eat together, making small talk.
We watch a football game, while you teach me the rules.

You and the boys try to figure out who's in the play-offs.
      (I watch you walk as you go to get the paper.)

You clean off the table.
      (Your sleeves are pushed up so I watch the muscles
       in your hands and forearms as you work.)

You pour us some wine and we all watch more TV.
      (I feel your soul acknowledge me as our bodies touch.
       Allowed now because they're engrossed in the show.)

Finally it is late enough for you and I to say we're tired.

The door to the bedroom clicks and...
      Parent quietly recedes.

Again you wake me with your snoring.
          But this time I don't mind.

The first time,
It took me several seconds
                              to realize what
                                        had awakened me.

Then I just shut you out.
And went back to sleep.

The second time,
I knew immediately
(What else could sound like that?).
When I rolled over and looked at you,
You were completely uncovered
                              except for
                                        one leg.
In the glow of the clock's face
          I could hardly keep from touching you.
So as not to wake you,
I touched your beard,
                              just once,
And went back to sleep.

The third time,
As I turned in your direction,
                              you awoke
Enough to scratch your chest.
I couldn't resist touching your hand,
Then wanted you so much
          I didn't care if I woke you.
I found,
(To my delight)
That caressing your chest and belly
Stops your snoring.
Back to sleep,
                    again.

Now,
the fourth time,
I just lay here
              listening and watching
                            you sleep.

Soon I'll touch you...
And you'll move.
And quit snoring.
But for right now
I won't change a thing.

When I watch you sleep
I like:


The mound of your hip or
                    buns or
                    belly
The sound of you breathing
                    whistling
                    snorting
The way the sunlight makes the hair on your body
                    shine red and gold
The curve of your neck against your chest.

The chance to study your hands
The way your soft, gentle lips move in your sleep.

When we're at my house;
        The way the sunlight comes in through the window
                    and makes your skin
                    look pink and healthy
When we're at your house;
        The way the dawn's first light comes in through
                    the curtain and gives your skin
                    a bluish pallor.

The way your penis lays against your leg.

Staring at you without your being self-conscious.


These are some of the things
                    I'll remember.

I have a past lover call me.   He wants to talk
            about his wife
            about his kids
            about his job.

I say, "Come on over."
        (I need to know where my heart is with him to help
         me define where I am with you.)

He comes in and we sit on the floor and talk.

He kisses me
        and holds me
        and brushes his hands over my nipples.
            and my body responds.

I tell him he has to leave.
        and don't call me again.

I don't love you like I loved him.
But I don't love him like that, either, now.

It didn't help.
I still don't know how I feel about you.

We have been together much.
But we still don't listen well
                    to each other.

We bring to this relationship
All the "protections" we have devised
            Over the years
            From past relationships
                    and experiences.

Mine don't let me hear what you say
The way you mean it.
Yours don't let you say what you feel.

Even our small conversations
                    tend to become

                                        ponderous.

Two intelligent adults
Labor fruitlessly
Over insignificant "nothings".

These overwrought exchanges leave
Traps for future attempts.
Will it someday be
No longer worth trying?

I stop by where you work
Only to say "hi."
       I am unannounced,
       You are unprepared.
We go to a conference room
       With glass walls,
And try to look businesslike.
       You act like an animal;
       I laugh too much.

You say, "I guess you'd like a drink."
       (I hope you're being crude because
        you're nervous.)
I say, "I'll meet you."
When I get there,
You aren't.

I kill time in the stores
And decide to meet you at work.

All is forgiven.
You have just made the
                  Biggest Deal
                  your company has ever had!

At the bar
We get 3 for 1.
       Neither of us have eaten.
We join two of your friends.
We all talk for an hour.
They leave; we talk.

             Through a vague alcohol cloud.

Somehow,
I am added to the list of
People you love.
               With parents
               children
               one cousin
               ex-wife.

I open my mouth and
"I love you"
Flies out like a canary
Through an open door
  (Even though that poor
   dumb bird
   may end up catfood.)

You ask me to explain.
   Are you perplexed?
     cautious?
     eager?

I have begun to measure my other relationships
By how I feel about you.
   Intense,
     but not pervading;
   Comfortable,
     but not boring;
   Lusty,
     but not tawdry.

I can't read your reaction.

What have I done?

Because you are far away
I ramble on paper,
In anticipation of
Your expected return.
My thoughts become exposed,
Feelings show form,
My soul is vulnerable
To criticism from people
Who don't live in here.
A diary of this sort
Is as close as you can
                    be
To inside my skin.
Know me as I am,
Not as you would have me.

You like watching my aggression.

When we are with your friends
Somewhere in the conversation,
You always say,
     "This one
      can take care of herself."

This one.
Sounds like I'm
Part of a harem.

This one,
Is an able
Verbal sparring partner.

This one,
Was a winning scrapper
In grade school.

This one,
Never followed the crowd
When the crowd was wrong.

This one,
Pays the price
Of being different.

This one,
Is a lot like you.

You invite me to have supper
With you
      your parents
      your son.
I'm extremely flattered.
I accept.

The evening is comfortable.
I enjoy your family.
By knowing the generation
Before and after you,
I know you better.

When it is time for me
To leave,
You offer to start my car.
You've never done that before,
That I remember.

We go to a vacant room
To say good-by.
It's dark
And cozy.
So nice to be alone with you.

You hold me close
And tell me you're
Holding back,
Until I decide
Where I want to be.

Please don't.

Tell me you love me
      If you do.
Hold me close
      If you want to.
Call me often
      If you can.

Should I have been flattered?
Should I hold back?

You're an enigma.
I'm confused.

When I want you,
And can't get to you,
I placate myself
By writing letters
That parallel our lovemaking.

I have noticed that
The longer I know you,
The longer the letters become.

Letters that tell you
Where I'd rather be,
What I'd like to be doing.

Letters that remind you
How softly I can touch you,
How well I know your body.

Letters that would vaporize ice
Will be long remembered by you.

You say I'm holding back.
I know I'm protecting myself.
The openness that drew you
To me at first
Has lessened, now.

When I know you
Sleep with other women,
I feel I'm being compared.
I'm afraid to let you see
How I act
When I'm alone and
Fantasizing
                    about you:
        I get goosebumps and chills;
        I smile incessantly;
        I shake like a tribal dancer.
My insides turn around
in circles
                            and
                change colors!


But all you get to see is a smile

It's been a month since
We slept...
               together.

We have talked
       face to face
             and
      on the phone.
We have had drinks
         and
              dinner.
We have held hands
            and
       each other.

You have made love
With other women;
I have held other men.

But

I think of you often
And
You think of me.

Sometimes...
            when I think of you,
You even have clothes on.

Your outside gets washed
        brushed
        combed
        flossed
        sprayed
        pulled in
        pushed out
        cut off
        clipped
        filed
        picked
        poked
        scratched
        covered
        uncovered
        protected and
        bared
in your preparation to meet the world.

In moments you weren't prepared
I've seen the inside that's small
          dark
          withered
          stinking
          mean
          ugly and
          afraid,

accepted it
embraced it
and love it, too.

Let me.

Words can't convey:

The excitement I feel
Anticipating your arrival;

The way my stomach flutters
When you walk into the room;

The disappointment when
Your machine answers the phone;

The joy inside me
Walking with you on a windy day;

The tenderness
From watching you sleep;


How can I tell you
How much I care?

I'm in your horoscope
You tell me.

My curiosity simmers
                              the weeks
                              it takes you
To hunt
              down
              the magazine.

As you read it,
I learn about you.
You agree with what
The author
Has to say
              about you.

I hear inflections
In your voice
And learn about you.

A romance is predicted.
Mentally stimulating.
Long-term.
You thought of me.

And
I learn about you.

Too many weeks
Have passed
Since you held me
In the dark.

We just stand
And enjoy.

You kiss me
And I feel your beard
(How can it be so coarse
  When the rest of your hair
        is
        so soft?).

I put one hand on your
Shoulder,
One on your neck.
With my lips
I work my way
            down
            into
            your collar.

You pull me closer.

We've got to find
A different way
To say
Good-by.

Doesnt matter
Mad Hatter
Off the wall
Through it all
Be just me
Let you see
Scare you off
With a cough
Mistimed
Not rhymed
Part of it
Nippled tit
Bare ass
To amass
Tho it reeks
Not in weeks
Felt your thighs
Heard your sighs
Took a stand
Held your hand

Saw your woman
Set me roamin
Had to run
Not for fun
Prickly loss
Harbors dross
Hurt like Hell
Rang a bell
Deep inside
Neednt hide
Got my Self
Off the shelf
Dust it down
Go to town
Not too bad
Glad I had
Not a pox
Nor a box

Damn nice person
Write a verse on
Let her feel
Sense her Real
Watch her grow
Feel her go
Doesnt bend
Mustnt end
Is protection
Vivisection
Battles long
Could be wrong
Doesnt matter
Mad Hatter

I smelled Spring!

When I dial your number
To tell you,
I hear

        an odd beep.

A machine

        (not yours this time)
Tells me
Your phone has been disconnected.

As panic overwhelms me
I imagine you have moved to Florida.
It was all a hoax.
I've been a "sucker" again.

Then.
When I see you,
I just ask why.
You will never see
The way my Control

              pooled

At my feet.

There is some consolation
Even in this.

If I can't call you
The others can't, either.

When I get to your house,
I need to call home.

But your phone is still out.

You offer to tell me where there's a phone.

There is six inches of snow out there,
It's covered by ice.
the temperature is below freezing
And...
                    so am I!

Send me to a phone!?!
        You Jerk!

I feel myself ready for a fight.
        my body tenses
        my eyebrow raises
        my mouth drops
        my eyes widen

As I turn to face you,
You throw your head back

                            and laugh
                            ---full and throaty.


I've been set up.


I feel the energy drain
And I can laugh, too.

My picture comes off your wall
because "the others"
feel uneasy with it there.


(Is it supposed to comfort me---
knowing there's more than one?)


A bare ass on your wall,
and one under your hand.
Are you uneasy?

When I'm flashing flesh
on your bed
and see the wall where I'm not,
Makes me wonder ...

How many pussies puddled here
since mine?
Are the numbers important?
Is that why the picture came down?

I don't understand.

It's your wall.
Why can't you say,

"It stays."


?

Yesternight we were cold
As guests
In this strange bed.
A sleeping bag from the car
Brings more than warmth
As we snuggle beneath.

My body radiates heat
As the morning's
Yellow fingers
Open sleepy eyes.
You comment that I must
Be very happy;
You've never felt my body
Show Happy like this.

... Because
Your bed
Is often cold
For me.
Though the covers are heavy
And words of love
Live there.

Months ago
(A hundred years ago)
I vowed to Myself
"I won't let him
  Do it to me...

                        Again."

It's so easy to let him into my soul:
I love him.
I respect him.
I admire him.
I hate him!
He loves me so well:
                My mind
                and
                My body.
So quickly those memories
Override the intellect
When he's on top of me,
And nude.

I don't remember:
Him saying,
"I can't see you anymore.
  But let's be Friends."
The ANGER!
The Hurt.
The way my stomach
                Attacks itself
                And refuses food
                        for days afterward.
Sleepless nights.
Restless days.
When he's on top of me,
And nude.

"Do you want to make love?"
How can it be that
I hear myself
Say, "Yes"
Again?

God!   I love him!
When he's on top of me,
And nude

So I'll take my chances.
And enjoy him while I can.
Maybe, just maybe
He'll be on top of me
And nude
For a long time ...
This time.

It's hard to remember you're
    not Here,

                anymore.


Watching a movie
I turn to share a thought

          with you...

But somebody else sits beside me.
My thoughts stumble.
And words quickly reorganize
    realign
      like children going to recess
So what I wanted to say
Will make sense
      to this stranger
      who has taken your place
      at my side.


At the performance last night
I started to remark on the colors
        and sequence
Of the dancers
Because they gave me goosebumps.
You would have understood.


But you weren't there.


Quips, quotes, cartoons
That might make you laugh
     or ponder;
Times I want to call
    or write
    or lay my hand on your arm;
Waking in the wee hours
With missing you ubiquitous;
I'm keeping to myself.
Giving you the space
      you asked for.

I'm following the rules for:
"Getting Him Out of Your System."
I've changed my route home.
I don't much go where we went.
I try to run you out of my thoughts.
I try not to talk about you unless asked.
I try not to...
I try not..

I try.

In Celebration of the Death of Faeries

The death of hope
and its examples

It isn't cute to
Believe in faeries
When you're "grown up"
And dreams begin to
colour of pragmatism.

But faeries and dreams seldom die on their own.

Like drowning kittens
They must be held down
Until all shards of life
Are broken
And the corpse
Is discarded---
Added to the heap
Of other murdered dreams
And daily rubbish.

Santa and his elves develop
Bright, black, empty eyes,
The Easter Bunny's eggs
Begin to rot,
The Tooth Fairy becomes
A crone with nose & chin grappling
Where she has no teeth
Of her own.

And cease to exist

For those of us
Who reluctantly
Relinquish
The ability to believe.

So a toast, my friend,
To the smitten remains of:
Blind Santas
Bloody Easter Bunnies
And crippled Faeries
With wings plucked and stored
To build the gossamer dreams
Of children,

From we who can
No longer
See
Through children's
Eyes.

You are going
Back
To her


I care more about you
Than you want me to.
But that's my problem.


I wish you Happy.

Made in the USA
Monee, IL
17 April 2022